Deutsche Grammatik niet- und nagelfest

Deutsche Grammatik niet- und nagelfest

Shannon Keenan Greene

Kuhn Publishing

Kuhn Publishing

Deutsche Grammatik niet- und nagelfest. 2nd Ed.
Shannon Keenan Greene. Kuhn, 2014.

© 2014, Kuhn Publishing

ISBN: 978-0-9905652-7-7

Table of Contents

Conjugation

Conjugation applies only to verbs, never to nouns. It has to do with having different endings on the verbs depending on who is doing the action of the verb: I <u>run</u> a marathon every year *versus* He <u>runs</u> a marathon every year.

English has verb conjugation, but it has all but died out over the centuries.

I live	we live
~~thou livest~~ (This form has died out)	you'all live (you-plural)
he/she/it live<u>s</u>	they live, You live

In English, we say he/she/it live<u>s</u>. The –<u>s</u> ending is a verb conjugation ending.

In German:

ich wohn<u>e</u>	wir wohn<u>en</u>
du wohn<u>st</u>	ihr wohn<u>t</u>
er/sie/es wohn<u>t</u>	sie wohn<u>en</u> / Sie wohn<u>en</u>

"du"=you, informal   "Sie"= you, formal

Notice the underlined endings in the chart above. These are verb conjugation endings.

a.wohnen

Du b.wohnt   in Deutschland.

c. wohnst

Only c. the –<u>st</u> ending is correct: Du wohn<u>st</u> in Deutschland.

"sie" can mean she or they. Why would any language have the same word for she and they? That is a good question and it is confusing. Only verb conjugation endings will tell you whether it's she or they (look at the conjugation chart above and find two instances of lowercase "sie")

sie wohn<u>t</u> in Berlin - sie must be "she" because of the verb ending (-t)

sie wohn<u>en</u> in Berlin - sie must be "they" because of the –en ending

Sie meaning "you" is always capitalized and takes the -en endings, so you is easy to confuse with they. If it's capitalized, then Sie means You.

Is it she, they, or You?

ich -<u>e</u>	wir -<u>en</u>
du -<u>st</u>	ihr -<u>t</u>
er/sie/es -<u>t</u>	sie -<u>en</u> / Sie -<u>en</u>

1. sie wohnt
2. sie wohnen
3. sie geht
4. Sie gehen
5. sie bringen
6. Sie bringen
7. sie glaubt

Answers

1. she
2. they
3. she
4. You
5. they
6. You
7. she

Conjugation / Additional practice

gehen-to go	
Ich geh**e**	wir geh**en**
du geh**st**	ihr geh**t**
er/sie/es geh**t**	sie geh**en** / Sie geh**en**

bringen-to bring	
Ich bring**e**	wir bring**en**
du bring**st**	ihr bring**t**
er/sie/es bring**t**	sie bring**en** / Sie bring**en**

glauben-to believe	
Ich glaub**e**	wir glaub**en**
du glaub**st**	ihr glaub**t**
er/sie/es glaub**t**	sie glaub**en** / Sie glaub**en**

What's the correct conjugation ending?

1. Thomas wohn_____ in Hamburg.

2. Ich glaub____ nicht alles. ("I don't believe everything.")

3. Stefanie bring_____ das Wasser für unseren Picknick.

4. Sie (she) wohn_____ in Stuttgart.

5. Sie (they) bring_____ Musik zu der Party.

Please translate:

1. they go-   sie _____
2. he believes –   er_____
3. I am bringing (same as "I bring")-   ich_____
4. we believe
5. I live (use "wohnen")
6. she brings
7. you (du) live
8. you (Sie) believe

Answers

1. -t
2. -e
3. -t
4. -t
5. —en

1. sie gehen
2. er glaubt
3. ich bringe
4. wir glauben
5. ich wohne
6. sie bringt
7. du wohnst
8. Sie glauben

Infinitives and verb stems

Examples of German verbs are:

> wohnen – to live
> gehen – to go
> sagen – to say

German verbs end in –en. The basic form of the verb has the –en ending and is called the infinitive.

In order to conjugate a verb, you remove the –en so that you just have just the stem of the verb, and then you add the conjugation endings to the stem:

gehen-to go	the infinitive is: **gehen**	
	the stem is: **geh-**	
Ich geh**e**	wir geh**en**	
du geh**st**	ihr geh**t**	
er/sie/es geh**t**	sie geh**en** / Sie geh**en**	

The **infinitive** is an important grammar concept with many uses.

The "stem" is an ad-hoc, made-up grammar concept based on the infinive (minus the –en). The stem is a useful concept for conjugation.

Helping verbs such as "I can…" do not usually stand alone. Instead, they are combined with a second, main verb. When this happens, **the helping verb is conjugated and the second verb is not conjugated. The second verb remains in the infinitive.**

Du <u>kannst</u> Deutsch **sprechen.** – You can speak German.
Wir <u>sollen</u> unsere Arbeit **machen.** – We should do our work.
Tim und Ute <u>können</u> Türkisch **verstehen** – Tim and Ute can understand Turkish.

Some infinitives do not end in –en:
> sein (stem **sei-**)
> wandern (stem **wander-**)

sie verste<u>hen</u> – they understand:
notice that the –en can be a conjugation ending

Is the word or fragment below a verb infinitive, a verb stem, or a conjugated form of the verb?
1. sagst
2. hab-
3. komme
4. wander-
5. sagen

Answers:

1. conjugated form
2. stem
3. conjugated form
4. stem
5. infinitive OR conjugated form. Below you will see one example of each:
   Ich <u>kann</u> "hallo" <u>sagen</u>. (sagen is the verb infinitive)
   <u>Wir sagen</u> oft "hallo". (sagen has the –en ending to agree with wir)

Gender

Gender applies to nouns only. It has nothing to do with verbs.

There are 3 genders in German: masculine, feminine, and neuter.

The way to say the word "the" is der (masc), **die** (fem), **das** (neut)

The way to say "a" or "an" is: ein (masc), **eine** (fem), **ein** (neut)

For every noun, the gender has to be memorized.

What is the gender of each noun? Please use a dictionary or www.leo.org. Answers are on the next page.

1. Buch
2. Mann
3. Kind
4. Tafel
5. Idee
6. FuBball
7. Besprechung – meeting

- Nouns that end in **–in, -ung,** or **-tion** are almost always feminine.
- Nouns that end in **–er** are almost always masculine. (But "Mutter"/mother und "Schwester"/sister are exceptions)
- Nouns that end in **–chen** are neuter

-in turns a noun into a feminine noun:

> Student – student; **Studentin – female student**
> Professor-professor; **Professorin – female professor**
> Freund-friend; **Freundin – female friend**

Change each phrase from "the" to "a":

1. die Tür (answer: *eine Tür*)
2. das Haus
3. der Student
4. die Idee – the idea
5. der Hund – the dog

Answers:

1. neut
2. masc
3. neut
4. fem
5. fem
6. masc
7. fem

1. eine
2. ein
3. ein
4. eine
5. ein

Gender and New Vocabulary

Masculine Nouns:

der Tisch-the table
der Mann-the man
der Hund-the dog
der Computer-the computer
der Euro- the euro (money/currency)
der FuBballspieler – the soccer player
der MP3-Spieler ("emm-pay-dry") – the MP3 player

Feminine Nouns:

die Arbeit-the work
die Tür-the door
die Freundin-the girlfriend
die Frau-the woman
die Uhr-the clock or the watch
die Idee-the idea
die Maus-the mouse

Neuter Nouns:

das Boot-the boat
das Mobiltelefon or das Handy – the cell phone
das Buch – the book
das Musikinstrument – the musical instrument
das Mädchen – the girl   ("little maid" / **-chen** means "little")

der, die or das?
Remember:
- Nouns that end in **–in, -ung,** or **-tion** are almost always feminine.
- Nouns that end in **–er** are almost always masculine. (But "die Mutter"/mother und "die Schwester"/sister are exceptions)
- Nouns that end in **–chen** are neuter

1. Buch
2. Uhr
3. Euro
4. Handy
5. Laptop-Computer
6. Musikinstrument
7. Mädchen
8. Besprechung-meeting
9. Schwester-sister
10. Nation
11. Freundin
12. Studentin

Answers

1.	das	7.	das
2.	die	8.	die
3.	der	9.	die
4.	das	10.	die
5.	der	11.	die
6.	das	12.	die

Plurals

In English, the plural is formed by adding –s to a noun. In German, -s is usually a genitive ending, which shows possession.

For each German noun, you have to memorize how to make the plural. There are some tendencies that can be helpful.

Maculine nouns: The plural is most likely to be **–e** but there are many exceptions.

> Hund- dog
> Hund**e**-dogs

Feminine Nouns: The plural is most likely to be **–n or –en** but there are many exceptions.

Neuter nouns: The plural may be **–er, -e,** or you might form the plural by **adding an Umlaut to one of the vowels in the word, plus an ending:**

> Haus- house
> Häus**er**-houses

A dictionary will tell you a noun's gender, and how to form the plural.

Many words borrowed from French or English have –s as the plural.

Go to www.leo.org and find the plural for each noun:

1. Tisch
2. Tür (type "Tuer" into the dictionary at leo.org)
3. Fisch
4. Wand - wall
5. Kind
6. Decke – blanket
7. Auto

Translate, using the list above:

1. Die _____ sind beige. (walls) – The walls are beige.
2. Ihre _____ sind sehr schön! (children) – Your children are very beautiful.
3. Die _____ sind aus isländischer Wolle. (blankets)-The blankets are made of Icelandic wool.

*"die" means "the" in the plural for all genders: _die_ is for masculine nouns in the plural, feminine nouns in the plural, and neuter nouns in the plural.
 (please note, feminine "the" and plural "the" are the same! they're both "die")

Answers:

1. Tische
2. Türen
3. Fische
4. Wände
5. Kinder
6. Decken
7. Autos

1. Wände
2. Kinder
3. Decken

Direct Objects

Look at pronouns in English. They change depending on whether they are the <u>subject</u> or the <u>direct object</u>:

Subject:	I	you	he	she	it	we	you	they	You
Direct Object: (also called Accusative)	me	you	him	her	it	us	you	them	You

Let's see what a direct object is by looking at two sentences in English:

1. The soldier started the jeep.
2. The jeep started the soldier.

In English, the <u>subject</u> of a sentence "the soldier" has to be the first element. Word order isn't optional. Why? Because sentence #2 above is confusing. How do you know who is doing the starting and who or what is receiving the action of the verb (that is, what is being started)? It's just not clear in sentence #2.

In German the subject (doing the action) has one word for the word "the" and the direct object (the thing that the soldier is starting) has a different word for "the." That way, you always know which word is the subject and which word is the direct object.

Der Soldat startet **den** Jeep.
Der Student startet **den** Computer.

When it's the subject of the verb:	When it's the direct object of the verb:
der Soldat	den Soldat
der Jeep	den Jeep
der Tisch-table	den Tisch
der Hund	den Hund
der Euro	den Euro

Underline the direct object of each verb:

1. The soldier picked up his Rucksack (backpack).
2. We have several cousins in that county.
3. My bicycle has a wobbly basket.
4. I know him!

Is each word below the <u>subject</u> or the <u>direct object</u>?

1. den Mann
2. der Laptop
3. der Euro
4. den Regenschirm-umbrella
5. der Porsche 911
6. den Tiger

Answers

1. The soldier picked up <u>his Rucksack</u> (backpack).
2. We have <u>several cousins</u> in that county.
3. My bicycle has <u>a wobbly basket</u>.
4. I know <u>him</u>!

1. direct object	3. subject	5. subject
2. subject	4. direct object	6. direct object

Accusative

The accusative is primarily used to identify and mark a noun phrase in a sentence that is not the subject, but is instead the direct object of the verb.

Der dritte Mann hat **einen Hund.** – The third man has a dog.

"**einen Hund**" is accusative in the sentence above, because it is the **direct object of the verb.**

"Accusative" applies to <u>the entire noun phrase</u>, not just the noun.

A pronoun takes the place of an entire noun phrase, so a pronoun can also be accusative. **Here are the pronouns:**

Subject	ich-I	du	er	sie	es	wir	ihr	sie	Sie
Direct Object /Accusative:	mich- me	dich	ihn	sie	es	uns	euch	sie	Sie

Prepositions (*in, on, next to, over, with, to*) always "take a case" in German. Some prepositions "take the accusative:

through, without, against, for, around

After the word "through" (or without, against, for, around), a noun phrase or a pronoun will follow. That noun phrase or pronoun has to be in the accusative:

durch den Wald – through the forest
ohne den Hund – without the dog
für mich – for me

Underline the direct object of the verb and write down what case it is in:

1. Ich habe einen braunen Hund.
2. Mein bester Freund hat einen Dell-Computer.
3. Ich will dieses Buch kaufen. – I want to buy this book.
4. Ich kenne dich! – I know you!

Underline the object of the preposition and write down what case it is in:
1. für Sie
2. um die Stadt
3. durch den Spiegel – through the looking glass

Why are all the noun phrases or pronouns above in the accusative?

Answers:

1. Ich habe <u>einen braunen Hund.</u>
2. Mein bester Freund hat <u>einen Dell-Computer.</u>
3. Ich will <u>dieses Buch </u>kaufen. – I want to buy this book.
4. Ich kenne <u>dich</u>.

1. für <u>Sie</u>
2. um <u>die Stadt</u>
3. durch <u>den Spiegel</u>

All the underlined phrases above (1-4 and 1-3) are accusative.

1-4 are all accusative because they are direct objects

1-3 are all accusative because they follow a preposition that is designated as being an "accusative preposition"

Accusative Prepositions

Matching column:

1.	für sie	a.	for me
2.	durch den Wald	b.	for us
3.	für mich	c.	for you (informal "you": du-form)
4.	ohne ihn	d.	through the forest
5.	für dich	e.	for You
6.	für uns	f.	without him
7.	für Sie	g.	for her

Subject	ich	du	er	sie	es	wir	ihr	sie	Sie
Direct Object /Accusative:	mich	dich	ihn	sie	es	uns	euch	sie	Sie

"für" takes the accusative case

It's for no logical reason; it's not the direct object of the verb which is what the accusative word endings are usually used for. It's actually the "object of a preposition."

It's simply an arbitrary rule: after "für," the next word will be treated as though it were a direct object. The next word will be in the accusative case.

Using the chart above, please translate:

1. for him
2. for me
3. for them
4. for you (Sie-form)
5. for you (du-form)

	masc.	fem.	neut.
The subject	der	die	das
The accusative	den	die	das

1. for the woman   für _____ Frau
2. for the computer   für _____ Computer
3. for the girl (neut.) für_____Mädchen
4. for the new man   für _____ neuen Mann

Just like für, several other prepositions also take the accusative:

durch, ohne, gegen, für, um – through, without, against, for, around

Answers

1. g
2. d
3. a
4. f
5. c
6. b
7. e

1. für ihn
2. für mich
3. für sie
4. für Sie
5. für dich

1. die
2. den
3. das
4. den

Articles

Articles precede nouns. Together they form a noun phrase: **the** bicycle, **a** house

> The word "a" or "an" is an article.
> The word "the" is also an article.

In English grammar terms, "a" or "an" is the indefinite article; "the" is the definite article. However, German grammar pedagogy uses different terminology.

Is an article an adjective? Sort of, yes; depending on how you model your grammar. But in German grammar or English grammar it makes more sense to say no.
There are special rules that only apply to articles. There are complicated endings just for articles. It's best to think of articles as not being adjectives.

What do articles express? In English or German, the indefinite article refers to <u>any</u> example of that noun **("a house," "a farmer")** whereas the definite article is a <u>specific</u> example of that noun: **"the university"** or **"the desk"** (a particular desk).

the word "the"

There are 16 ways to say "the," depending on the gender, number (sing. or plur.) and case of the noun:

"the"

The 4 cases:	masc	fem	neut	plural
nomimative	der	die	das	die
accusative	den	die	das	die
dative (you haven't learned this yet)	dem	der	dem	den
genitive (you haven't learned this yet)	des	der	des	der

There is a similar chart for "a/an."

All articles are divided into: der-words and ein-words. The der-words take endings like the chart above. You will learn more about this later.

Underline the articles (the, or a/an) in the paragraph below. Two roommates are sharing a refrigerator. There is a translation on the next page if you need it.

Kai:	Hallo, Markus, wo ist die Milch?
Markus:	Ich habe Milch für mein Müsli gebraucht.
Kai:	Hast du einen ganzen Karton gebraucht?
Markus:	Na ja, du hast noch eine Flasche Wein.
Kai:	*Meine* Flasche Wein, ja. Aber ich will den Wein im Moment nicht. Ich will ein Glas Milch trinken. Schon gut. Ich trinke eine Cola.
Markus:	Ich habe gestern eine Flasche Cola getrunken. War es deine Cola?

Translation

Kai:	Hi, Markus, where is the milk?
Markus:	I needed (have needed) milk for my müsli (a kind of breakfast cereal).
Kai:	Did you need a whole carton?
Markus:	Oh well, you still have a bottle of wine.
Kai:	*My* bottle of wine, yes. But at the moment I don't want the wine. I want to drink a glass of milk. It's okay. I'll trink a soda (cola, pop).
Markus:	Yesterday I drank a bottle of cola. Was it yours?

Answers

Kai:	Hallo, Markus, wo steht <u>die</u> Milch?
Markus:	Ich habe Milch für mein Müsli gebraucht.
Kai:	Hast du <u>einen</u> ganzen Karton gebraucht?
Markus:	Na ja, du hast noch <u>eine</u> Flasche Wein.
Kai:	*Meine* Flasche Wein, ja. Aber ich will <u>den</u> Wein im Moment nicht. Ich will <u>ein</u> Glas Milch trinken. Schon gut. Ich trinke <u>eine</u> Cola.
Markus:	Ich habe gestern <u>eine</u> Flasche Cola getrunken. War es deine Cola?

*mein and dein are called "ein-words" (words that behave gramatically like "ein") They are technically not articles, but in a later unit this will be explained more clearly.

Possessive Adjectives

Possessive adjectives show possession:

my(**mein**), your(**dein**), his(**sein**), her(**ihr**), their(**ihr**), Your(**Ihr**)

These words **take endings that show case** similar to the way the word "ein" takes endings and changes: ein, eine, ein; einen, eine, ein; einem, etc.

Let's review the endings for **a/an**:

"ein" ("a/an")

	masc	fem	neut	plural
nomimative	ein	eine	ein	
accusative	einen	eine	ein	

The endings on mein(my), dein(your), sein(his), etc. are the same endings. That's why they're called "ein-words": they decline (take endings) just like "ein"

"mein" ("my")

	masc	fem	neut	plural
nomimative	mein	meine	mein	
accusative	meinen	meine	mein	

Let's decline "dein" using a full 4 X 4 chart, including the two cases we haven't learned yet (dative and genitive), and let's fill out the plural too.

"dein" ("your" / informal)

	masc	fem	neut	plural
nomimative	dein	deine	dein	deine
accusative	deinen	deine	dein	deine
dative	deinem	deiner	deinem	deinen
genitive	deines	deiner	deines	deiner

Any ein-word will decline exactly like the chart above. (To "decline" means to take case endings. Verbs conjugate, noun phrases decline.)

The ein words are ein, kein, and the possessive adjectives. In other words:

ein	**sein**
kein	**ihr**
mein	**ihr**
dein	**Ihr**

Following the chart for "dein" above, and keeping in mind that all ein-words have the same endings, write a 4 X 4 chart for "Ihr" meaning "Your" (formal)

Answers

"Ihr" ("Your")

	masc	fem	neut	plural
nomimative	Ihr	Ihre	Ihr	Ihre
accusative	Ihren	Ihre	Ihr	Ihre
dative	Ihrem	Ihrer	Ihrem	Ihren
genitive	Ihres	Ihrer	Ihres	Ihrer

*The main point to glean from this chapter is that words decline (take endings) all "ein-words" decline the same way, and ein, kein, and the possessive adjectives (my-your-his-etc.) are all ein-words.

The actually endings won't make sense to you until we learn all the cases, but try to get a feel for the big picture: there is a group called "ein-words," and they all take the same endings for the different cases.

Prepositions

A preposition *(to, from, over, before, with)* together with a noun phrase forms a prepositional phrase.

What case should the noun phrase be in after a preposition? Accusative? Nominative?

The answer is: it depends on the preposition.

> **Accusative prepostions** take the accusative case.
> **Dative prepositions** take the dative case.
> **Genitive prepositions** (which are rare) take the genitive case.

There are no nominative prepositions.

Accusative prepositions are: durch, ohne, gegen, für, um

Dative prepositions are: aus, außer, bei, mit, nach, seit, von, zu

Genitive prepositions are: trotz, wegen, während

Place "mich" after each accusative prepositions and "mir" after each dative preposition. Then translate the phrase.

1. für
2. außer
3. bei
4. von
5. ohne
6. mit
7. nach

Answers:

1. für mich – for me
2. auBer mir – except for me
3. bei mir – at my house
4. von mir – from me
5. ohne mich – without me
6. mit mir – with me
7. nach mir – after me

Separable-Prefix Verbs

1. I wake up at 8 am.
2. I wake at 8 am up. – Ich wache um 8 Uhr auf.

"wake up" is a verb in two parts. #1 above is correct in English. #2 is correct in German, because in German, the "prefix" or smaller word (usually smaller) goes to the end of the sentence.

I <u>get up</u> from the sofa. (English: prefix stays with the verb)
Ich <u>stehe</u> vom Sofa <u>auf</u>. (German: prefix at the end of the sentence)

> ich wache auf – I wake up
> du stehst auf – you get up (from bed, from a chair…)
> er kommt mit – he's coming along (he's coming with us)

The infinitive forms of these verbs are:

aufwachen or auf-wachen– to wake up
aufstehen – to arise, to get up
mitkommen – to come along, to come with

Please fill in the blanks.

"What are you bringing along?"
> Was _____ du _____? (mit-bringen)

"The data are finally coming together":
> Die Datei_____ endlich mal _____. (zusammen-kommen)

"Please go up the stairs":
> _____ Sie bitte die Treppe _____. (hinauf-gehen)

Answers

Was <u>bringst</u> du <u>mit</u>?
Die Datei <u>kommen</u> endlich mal <u>zusammen</u>.
<u>Gehen</u> Sie bitte die Treppe <u>hinauf</u>.

Helping Verbs and Modal Verbs

Modal verbs are really helping verbs, but somehow a technical term used by grammarians made its way into a lot of ordinary German textbooks.

A helping verb combines with another verb:
I want to go; I can help, We must hurry, They can speak German really well.

The helping verbs in the sentences above are: I want, I can, We must, etc. **A helping verb usually needs another verb in order to complete the action of the verb:**

I want … to go. "want" is the helping verb and "to go" is the infinitive.

Helping verbs (modal verbs) aren't really very complicated, because they function in the same ways in English or German. **Always conjugate the helping verb**. It should have an ending that agrees with the subject.

Don't conjugate the other verb (the "main verb"). It stays in the **infinitive form.**

> **müssen – to have to, must**
> **können – to be able to, can, to be capable of doing something**
> **wollen – to want to**
> **sollen – should**

möchten – is technically not a verb; it's a form of mögen. But it functions like a helping verb:

Ich **möchte** eine Pizza bestellen – I'd like to order a pizza

Ich will – means "I want to" (not "I will") Notice there is no –e ending. Modal verbs and helping verbs often conjugate irregularly!

Ich werde – means "I am going to" or "I will": In other words, "Ich werde" creates the future tense.

Conjugate the verb in parentheses to agree with the subject or else leave it in the infinitive: whichever is correct.

1. Ich _____ jetzt mit euch ausgehen. Meine Arbeit ist fertig. (können)
2. Du sollst mit deinem Arzt _____. Du bist sehr erkältet. (sprechen)
3. Ich _____ ein neues Auto kaufen. (wollen-be careful; it is an irregular verb)

Now go to http://de.wiktionary.org and (partially) conjugate <u>one</u> of the helping verbs in the gray box above:

ich	
du	
er/sie/es	

Answers

1. kann
2. sprechen
3. will

ich	will
du	willst
er/sie/es	will

ich	muss
du	musst
er/sie/es	muss

ich	soll
du	sollst
er/sie/es	soll

ich	kann
du	kannst
er/sie/es	kann

ich	werde
du	wirst
er/sie/es	wird

Stem-Changing Verbs

Some verbs conjugate irregularly. You may notice patterns, but you basically have to memorize irregular verbs.

lesen-to read

ich lese	wir lesen
du liest	ihr lest
er/sie/es liest	sie/Sie lesen

sprechen-to speak

ich spreche	wir sprechen
du sprichst	ihr sprecht
er/sie/es spricht	sie/Sie sprechen

fahren-to drive, to travel by vehicle including car or train

ich fahre	wir fahren
du fährst	ihr fahrt
er/sie/es fährt	sie/Sie fahren

Please fill in the blanks below:

1. Du _____ sehr gut Deutsch.(sprechen)
2. Du _____ ein bisschen langsam. (fahren)
3. Wie oft _____ Hans Englisch? (sprechen)
4. Anna und Sabine _____ gern Krimis. (lesen)

Answers

1. sprichst
2. fährst
3. spricht
4. lesen

Dative

The German dative means **"to" or "for"** and is characterized by the endings **–m** (for masc and neut) and **–r** (for feminine).

In a sentence, the subject of the verb is in the nominitive case and has nominative endings. The direct object, if there is one, is in the accusative case and has accusative endings. **The indirect object, if there is one, is in the dative case and has dative endings.**

Look at the **indirect object** below:

> I gave my brother a video game.

"my brother" is the indirect object. To test it, does it make sense to say "to my brother" or "for my brother"? If so, then it is the indirect object.

> I showed my friends my new laptop.
> I bought my roommate a red lamp.
> Give me a chance to show you the quality of my work.
> I gave my parents a book about art.

Using the "to/for" test, underline the indirect objects above.

Here are the answers: *my friends, my roommate, me, you, my parents*

The dative shows indirect objects. The dative endings are:

"der-die-das" ("the")

	masc	fem	neut	plural
dative	dem	der	dem	den

For ein-words such as ein, kein, mein, dein, sein, etc. let's use sein- as an example:

"sein" ("his")

	masc	fem	neut	plural
dative	seinem	seiner	seinem	seinen

Er gibt <u>seinem Onkel</u> ein gutes Buch zu Weihnachten. – He's giving <u>his uncle</u> a good book for Christmas.

Put each indirect object below into the dative case:

1. Peter gibt _____ ein Videospiel zu Weihnachten. (sein Bruder)
2. Uwe gibt _____ ein Fahrrad. (seine Tante – his aunt)
3. Willi gibt _____ einen Gutschein. (der Automechaniker)

Answers

1. seinem Bruder
2. seiner Tante
3. dem Automechaniker

How often do indirect objects arise? Not so often. Not as often as subjects (which are in every sentence) or direct objects (which are frequent).

The primary use of the dative case in beginner and intermediate German is as the object of Dative Prepositions. To learn more, begin reading the next unit.

Dative prepositions

The dative prepositions are: **aus (from, out of), auBer(except for), bei(at the house of), mit(with), nach(after; toward,to), seit(since), von(from), zu(to)**

The dative <u>pronouns</u> are:

Nominative	ich	du	er	sie	es	wir	ihr	sie	Sie
Accusative	mich	dich	ihn	sie	es	uns	euch	sie	Sie
Dative	mir	dir	ihm	ihr	ihm	uns	euch	ihnen	Ihnen

Translate the phrases below:

1. with me
2. from them
3. except for him
4. after you (Sie form)
5. after you (du form)
6. with her
7. from you (du form)

"der-die-das"("the")

	masc	fem	neut	plural
dative	dem	der	dem	den

Translate the phrases below:

1. from the house (das Haus)
2. from the school (die Schule)
3. to the doctor (zu / der Arzt)
4. except for the soccer ball

Answers:

1. mit mir
2. von ihnen
3. außer ihm
4. nach Ihnen
5. mit dir
6. mit ihr
7. von dir

1. von dem Haus
2. von der Schule
3. zu dem Arzt (can be abbreviated as zum Arzt; zum is a contraction of zu dem)
4. außer dem Fußball

Dative with der-words and ein-words

Remember, the dative endings are –m (masc. and neut.) or –r (fem.)

Typical German!

1. Ich spiele oft Tischtennis mit mein_____ Schwester.
2. Ich spiele FuBball mit mein_____ Freund Bastian und sein_____ Bruder Gerhard. (his brother Gerhard)
3. Ich singe gern in d___ Kneipe mit mein_____ Freund Stefan. (die Kneipe=the bar, the pub)
4. Ich arbeite mit mein___ Cousine (female cousin) zusammen in ein_____ Fabrik. (die Fabrik=the factory)
5. Ich esse jeden Sonntag (every Sunday) mit mein_____ Vater und mit mein_____ Mutter zusammen bei ihnen (at their house).

die Ecke	the corner
der Garten	the garden
das Haus	the house
das Wohnzimmer	the living room
die Garage	the garage
die Werkstatt	the auto mechanic's repair shop
das Kapitel	the chapter

1. Ich habe eine grüne Sofa in mein__ Wohnzimmer.
2. Der neue Gartengnome steht in ein___ Ecke in d_____ Garten hinter d_____ Haus.
3. Ich kann nicht fahren. Mein Auto ist nicht in d___ Garage. Es ist in d___ Werkstatt.
4. Ich habe eine Frage über die Hausaufgabe. In d___ zweiten Kapitel auf Seite 42 (zweiundvierzig) gibt es einen Satz, den ich nicht genau verstehe.(a sentence that I don't exactly understand)

42

Answers

1. er
2. em, em
3. er, em
4. er, er
5. em, er

1. em
2. er, em, em
3. er, er
4. em

Two-Way Prepositions

The German preposition **"in"** sometimes takes the accusative and sometimes takes the dative.

When it means "into" it takes the accusative:

> Let's go **into** the movie theater. (the movie theater will be accusative)
> Max walked **into** the forest. (the forest will have accusative endings)

When it means "in" and does not show motion into something (motion toward a goal), then it takes dative.

I have a billiard room **in** my house. (my house takes dative endings: in meinem Haus)
There's a gnome **in** my garden. (my garden takes dative endings: in meinem Garten)

Here is a reminder of the case endings:

	masc	fem	neut	plural
nomimative	der	die	das	die
accusative	den	die	das	die
dative	dem	der	dem	den

"the"

Does each phrase mein "in" or "into"?

1. in meinem Garten
2. in meinen Garten
3. in das Kino
4. in dem Kino
5. in der Schule
6. in die Schule
7. in den Laden (der Laden-the store)

Answers

1. in
2. into
3. into
4. in
5. in
6. into
7. into

Including "in" there are a total of 9 two-way prepositions:

an, auf, hinter, in, neben, über, unter, vor, zwischen

Using these correctly is a very advanced level skill, but you should just be aware that they exist. As a shortcut…they're usually dative.

Genitive

The genitive case expresses possession and looks like this:

	masc	fem	neut	plural
genitive	des … -es	der	des … -es	der

> der Name **des Mannes** – the name of the man (the man's name)
> der Name **des Kindes** – the name of the child

Use **des** for masc and neut, and also add **–es** to the noun. However, if the noun is more than one syllable long, then use des … -s: **des Ingenieurs** – *of the engineer*

Translate into German:

1. the name of the director (der Direktor)
2. the name of the institute (das Institut)
3. the dog's name (first, start by changing it to "the name of the dog")

For feminine nouns (of the lady, of the university) there is no –(e)s on the noun. Use "der" to mean "of the":

Der Vorname **der Frau** ist Pia. – The woman's first name is Pia.

Translate:

1. of the house
2. of the engineer (masc)
3. of the university (die Universität)
4. of the cat (die Katze)
5. of the game (das Spiel)

Answers

1. der Name des Direktors
2. der Name des Instituts
3. der Name des Hundes

1) des Hauses
2) des Ingenieurs
3) der Universität
4) der Katze
5) des Spieles

The Four Cases

Case applies to a noun phrase (or a pronoun). It shows the role that the noun phrase is playing within the logic of a sentence. Is it the subject? Is it the direct object? Is it the indirect object? Does it show possession as in "the color of the laptop sleeve"?

For the most part, German expresses case by adding an ending onto the articles (The articles are the der-words and the ein-words). For example:

"the"

The 4 cases:	masc	fem	neut	plural
nomimative	der	die	das	die
accusative	den	die	das	die
dative	dem	der	dem	den
genitive	des	der	des	der

The use of the four cases can be summarized like this:

	Use #1	Use #2
nominative	1. The subject of the sentence	2. after the verb "to be" Das ist der Mann. (nominative)
accusative	1. the direct object of the sentence	2. after accusative prepositions (durch, ohne, gegen, für, um)
dative	1. the indirect object of a sentence; meaning "to" or "for"	2. after dative prepositions (aus, auBer, bei, mit, nach, seit, von, zu)
genitive	1. to show possession; meaning "of the"	2. after genitive prepositions (während, wegen, trotz)

Which of the four cases is this?

1. It shows the direct object of a verb
2. It comes after the preposition "mit"
3. It shows possession
4. It has the endings: dem-der-dem
5. It shows the subject of the sentence; it's the most basic case
6. It comes after the preposition "für"
7. The pronouns look like this: mich-dich-ihn-sie-es-uns-euch-sie-Sie
8. The pronouns look like this: mir-dir-ihm-ihr-ihm-uns-euch-ihnen-Ihnen

Answers

1. accus
2. dat
3. gen
4. dat
5. nomin
6. accus
7. accus
8. dat

Past Tense – The Perfect

This is the basic way of expressing events that happened in the past. It called the "Perfect Tense" but what that really means is the Past Tense.

German has a two-part past tense: the **helping verb** (usually haben) plus something called the **Past Participle.**

> Ich **habe** einen guten Film **gesehen.** – I saw a good movie.

In the sentence above, "Ich habe … gesehen" means "I saw."

It is a **two-part** past tense: **haben** (conjugated to "ich habe" plus the **past participle** of the verb sehen- to see. **Every verb has exactly one past participle.** It's used (with a helping verb) to show the past tense.

Past Tense:

haben	**+**	Past Participle, *which is:*
(conjugated)		-t
ich habe, du hast,	ge- + Stem of the Verb +	*or*
er hat, …		-en

You can see the basic structure of a "Past Participle": ge- + Verb Stem + -t or –en However, it is best to **memorize the Past Participles of common verbs** rather than trying to construct them. For one thing, the stem may be irregular, and you won't know whether it ends in –t or –en until someone tells you.

Look up the past participle for each word below in http://de.wiktionary.org by finding the block that says "Perfekt" and looking under "Partizip II"

1. sagen
2. wohnen
3. sprechen
4. verstehen
5. hören
6. arbeiten
7. denken

Now, provide the helping verb (conjugated to agree with the subject) and the Past Partciple (use de.wiktionary.org if needed):

1. I listed to music all day: Ich _____ den ganzen Tag Musik _____. (hören)
2. Max understood the lesson: Max _____ die Lektion _____. (verstehen)
3. I saw my parents: Ich _____ meine Eltern _____. (sehen)

Answers

1. gesagt
2. gewohnt
3. gesprochen
4. verstanden
5. gehört
6. gearbeitet
7. gedacht

1. habe / gehört
2. hat / verstanden
3. habe / gesehen

The Past Tense with "sein"

Please see the previous unit which describes the so-called "Perfect Tense" (Past Tense). It expresses actions that occurred in the past and it is formed using a helping verb (haben) plus the Past Participle of the verb.

Sometimes the helping verb is not "haben" but rather "sein" which means "to be."

Do you know the Christmas Carol *Joy to the World*? It begins: "Joy to the world, the Lord **is** come." Why does it say "Is come" instead of "has come"? Because in older versions of English, the past tense of "to come" used "is" as the helping verb: not: "has come" but rather "is come." In modern German you still say "Der Herr (the Lord) ist gekommen".

Sarah **ist** um 19 Uhr nach Hause <u>gekommen</u>. – Sarah <u>came</u> home at 7 pm.

Ich **bin** am Freitag nach Hause <u>gegangen</u>. – I <u>went</u> home on Friday.

kommen, gehen, laufen, and **aufwachen** (to wake up) all take "sein" as their helping verb <u>in the past tense</u>.

Conjugation of sein (irregular):

sein – to be

ich bin –I am	wir sind-we are
du bist-you are	ihr seid-you'all are
er/sie/es ist-he/she/it is	sie sind-they are; Sie sind-you(formal) are

To use a verb in the past tense, you need to know two things:
1. what is the Past Participle?
2. does it take haben or sein as the helping verb in the past tense? Look up the verb "laufen" in de.wiktionary.org . It tells you the past participle for every verb. Does it also tell you the helping verb? (Hint: look at the Perfekt row) The answer should be yes. Now, use de.wiktionary to find the helping herbs and past participles below.

Verb (infinitive form)	haben or sein as a helping verb?	Past Participle
wohnen		
verstehen		
gehen		
laufen		
kaufen		
kommen		
aufwachen		

Answers

Verb (infinitive form)	haben or sein as a helping verb?	Past Participle
wohnen	haben	gewohnt
verstehen	haben	verstanden
gehen	sein	gegangen
laufen	sein	gelaufen
kaufen	haben	gekauft
kommen	sein	gekommen
aufwachen	sein	aufgewacht

Past Tense – The Simple Past or Preterite

German has two past tenses. The "Simple Past" or Preterite is archaic and is slowly falling out of use. The perfect tense is alive and well. There are many fashionable explanations about these two tenses in ways that may not be entirely accurate in actual use. The two tenses can often be used interchangeably, except that the preterite sounds old-fashioned and the perfect sounds more contemporary. In speaking, both tenses are used but **the perfect is more common**. Sometimes the simple past is used for very complicated sentences when the two-part perfect tense would be too convoluting. In writing, both tenses are used. The simple past or preterite is used for fairy tales, older literature, or for giving a story an old-fashioned feel. It's also used in modern writing; in fact, one sentence may contain both past tenses for no particular reason. Some verbs are almost never used in the preterite, others (such as "sein") are used only infrequently in the perfect.

The simple past of "sein" is often used in speaking and writing:

ich war	wir waren
du warst	ihr wart
er/sie/es war	sie waren
	Sie waren

The simple past of "haben" is also used frequently in speaking and writing:

ich hatte	wir hatten
du hattest	ihr hattet
er/sie/es hatte	sie hatten
	Sie hatten

Translate:

1. Zöe had a dog (don't forget: ei<u>nen</u> Hund)
2. Julian was a good soccer player (ein guter FuBballer)
3. I was in the gym. (in der Sporthalle or im FitneB-Studio)

Answers

1. Zöe hatte einen Hund.
2. Julian war ein guter FuBballer.
3. Ich war in der Sporthalle.

Future Tense

In German, you can use the present tense to express actions that you will be doing in the future.

> Ich gehe morgen nach Hause. – Tomorrow I (will) go home.

However, if you want to clarify explicitly that this is a future action in the future tense, then use the helping verb "werden".

The Future Tense:

> werden   +   Verb Infinitive
> (conjugated)   (at the end of the sentence)

In many languages, you have to memorize the future tense form for each verb. In German, just learn how to conjugate werden and use that as a helping verb. That's the entire future tense. It's actually the easiest tense to learn.

This is how "werden" is conjugated:

ich werde	wir werden
du wirst	ihr werdet
er/sie/es wird	sie werden Sie werden

> Ich **werde** meine Hausaufgaben am Morgen **machen** – *I will do my homework in the morning.*

In English, you can also express the future tense by saying "I am going to do my homework" – just make sure you use "werden" in the German version.

> I'm **going to** go for a walk. – Ich **werde** einen Spaziergang **machen.**

will =   werden
going to =   werden

Translate:

1. I'm going to buy an iPad (einen iPad).
2. Gerhard is going to learn English.
3. I will make coffee (Kaffee kochen) in the morning (am Morgen).

Answers

1. Ich werde einen iPad kaufen.
2. Gerhard wird Englisch lernen.
3. Ich werde am Morgen Kaffee kochen. *(You may change the word order "Kaffee am Morgen kochen", but make sure "kochen" is at the end of the sentence.)*

der-words

The word "the" can have 16 different forms, depending on the gender and the case. The same is true for the word "dieser" meaning "this."

"dieser"("this")

	masc	fem	neut	plural
nomimative	dieser	diese	dieses	diese
accusative	diesen	diese	dieses	diese
dative	diesem	dieser	diesem	diesen
genitive	dieses	dieser	dieses	dieser

Let's take the "dieser" endings and make a chart just for the endings:

"dieser" endings (also known as der-word endings)

	masc	fem	neut	plural
nomimative	—er	—e	—es	—e
accusative	—en	—e	—es	—e
dative	—em	—er	—em	—en
genitive	—es	—er	—es	—er

Certain words take "der-word endings":

> solcher- such
> mancher-many a
> welcher? – which?

Mancher Soldat ist nicht kampfbereit wenn ein Krieg ausbricht. – *Many a soldier is not ready for combat when a war breaks out.*

Mit **welchem Computer** arbeiten Sie? – Which computer are you working with?

Translate:
1. which Computer? (accusative case)
2. such happiness (das Glück) (nominative case)
3. many a night (accusative case)

Adjective Endings after der-words

What about nouns phrases with adjectives like "this intelligent approach (to project management)"? Well, if you know the gender of "approach," then you can use the chart above to put the correct ending on "this": **dieses intelligente Konzept.** You can also look up the adjective ending for "intelligent." In (advanced) German grammar, **adjectives get a special set of endings if that adjective follows a der-word.** That's why it's so important to know der-words.

Answers

1. welchen Computer?
2. solches Glück
3. manche Nacht

ein-words

In the last unit you learned what der-words are and what endings you need to put on der-words. Der-word endings are specific, giving you a lot of detailed information about gender and case. For example, if I hear the word "dem" or "diesem"(this), I know that the next word will be in the dative case, and it will be either masculine or neuter.

ein-words are also detailed with regard to gender and case, <u>but not quite as detailed as der-words are.</u> For example, if I say "ein Geschäft" you cannot know the gender of Geschäft or even what case it's in. **Der-word endings and ein-word endings are both very similar, but ein-word endings are slightly more "vague"** or underdetermined, however you want to say it.

When an adjective comes after an ein-word, the adjective will need to contain a slighly greater amount of grammatical information, in order to compensate for the vagueness of ein-word endings.

This means: adjectives get different endings, depending on whether an adjective follows an ein-word or follows a der-word. This is the most complicated concept in all of intermediate and advanced German, but it makes logical sense.

What are the 3 types of ein words?
(hint: ein, kein, and something else...)

1.
2.
3.

The ein-word endings are:

ein-word endings

	masc	fem	neut	plural
nomimative	—	—e	—	—e
accusative	—en	—e	—	—e
dative	—em	—er	—em	—en
genitive	—es	—er	—es	—er

Compared to the der-word endings in the previous unit, which three boxes (which three endings) in the chart above are different? How are they different?

Answers:

1. ein
2. kein
3. the possessive adjectives (mein, dein, sein, ihr, sein, unser, euer, ihr, Ihr)

	masc	fem	neut	plural
nomimative	-er versus [no ending]	—e	-es versus [no ending]	—e
accusative	—en	—e	-es versus [no ending]	—e
dative	—em	—er	—em	—en
genitive	—es	—er	—es	—er

Adjective Endings

That's an interesting project!
What's your new seminar like?
How is the old bicycle doing?
Have you heard from your German language exchange parner?
Green onions are called "scallions" in many regions.

The sentences above have a medley of ein-words, der-words, and adjectives. You know how to put endings on ein-words and der-words (if you can figure out the case and the gender, look at the ein-word chart or the der-word chart to find the endings), and now we'll learn how to put endings on **adjectives.**

The back story on adjective endings.

First of all, this will never be easy when speaking unless you work on your German for 5-10 years on average. Until then, adjective endings don't come naturally; they just don't. Our language family, the Indo-European languages, used to have incredibly complex ending systems with detailed different endings depending on case and gender. In addition, these endings were completely different for different classes of nouns: farm animals versus people for example declined in entirely different ways so you had to learn a whole new set of endings. These were ancient peoples with no writing system, and yet their grammar was incredibly complex! Languages from this family include German and English, Old Icelandic, Latin, Greek, Russian, Hindi, Farsi/Persian, Sanskrit, Swedish, Greek, and many others. There are two kinds of German: low and high German, depending on whether you live on the plains or in the mountains; standard German is "high" German. Old High German, Old English, Sanskrit, Ancient Greek, and Old Icelandic all have incredibly complex grammar systems, because they are older languages in this Indo-European family.

Let's get back to our German examples and identify each word as an ein-word, a der-word, or an adjective. You can look up adjective endings in a chart, but you have to be sensitive to the context of the adjective. Let's practice that first.

Is the underlined word a der-word, an ein-word, or an adjective?
Remember: the possessive anjectives (my, your...) are ein-words.

1. That's <u>an interesting</u> project!
2. What's <u>your new</u> seminar like?
3. How is <u>the old</u> bicycle doing?
4. Have you heard from <u>your German</u> language exchange parner?
5. <u>Green</u> onions are called "scallions" in many regions.

Answers

1. ein-word, adjective
2. ein-word, adjective
3. der-word, adjective
4. ein-word, adjective
5. adjective

Adjective Ending Charts

If an adjective comes after a **der-word** such as "the" it will get one set of endings and there is a chart where you can look up the ending. "the new film" and "this enhanced car engine" are examples. If an adjective comes after an **ein-word** such as "a" or "my" it will get a different set of endings and there will be a different chart. "a red umbrella" and "his old bicycle" are examples. If an adjective such as "German customs" or "good man!" **does not come after either a der-word or an ein-word**, it will have its own set of endings, and its own chart.

Adjective endings after der-words take these endings:

	masc	fem	neut	plur
nominative	e	e	e	en
accusative	en	e	e	en
dative	en	en	en	en
genitive	en	en	en	en

Adjective endings after ein-words take these endings:

	masc	fem	neut	plur
nominative	er	e	es	en
accusative	en	e	es	en
dative	en	en	en	en
genitive	en	en	en	en

Unpreceded adjectives (there is no der-word and no ein-word before the adjective) take these endings:

	masc	fem	neut	plur
nominative	er	e	es	e
accusative	en	e	es	e
dative	em	er	em	en
genitive	en	er	en	er

Provide the ending for each adjective below. Be sure to consult the correct chart above.

1. *"The new vehicle is working well.":*
   Der neu____ Wagen läuft gut. (nominative, masculine)
2. *"That's a good book":*
   Das ist ein gut____ Buch. (nominative, neuter)
3. *"I'm working together with a German engineer.":*
   Ich arbeite mit einem deutsch____ Ingenieur zusammen. (dative, masculine)
4. *"Austrian food is world-famous":*
   Österreichisch____ Essen ist weltbekannt. (nominative, neuter)

Answers

1. e
2. es
3. en
4. es

If you found this book helpful,
please consider purchasing other books from Kuhn Publishing &
other books by Shannon Keenan Greene.

Grow in knowledge, grow in strength, grow in soul.

www.ingramcontent.com/pod-product-compliance
Lightning Source LLC
Chambersburg PA
CBHW062115090426
42741CB00016B/3426